MANAGING
PEOPLE

ESSENTIAL
MANAGERS

MANAGING
PEOPLE

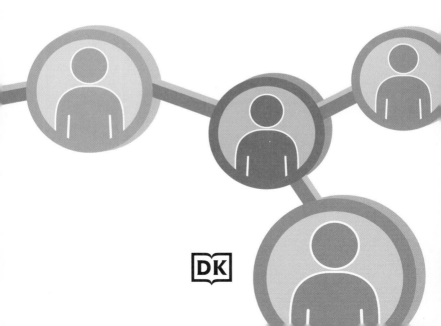

DK

Produced for DK by Dynamo Ltd
1 Cathedral Court, Southernhay East, Exeter, EX1 1AF

**Written by Philip L. Hunsaker and
Johanna Hunsaker**

Senior Art Editor Helen Spencer
Senior Editor Chauney Dunford
Jacket Design Development Manager Sophia MTT
Jacket Designers Akiko Kato, Juhi Sheth
Producer Nancy-Jane Maun
Production Editor Gillian Reid
Senior Managing Art Editor Lee Griffiths
Managing Editor Gareth Jones
Associate Publishing Director Liz Wheeler
Art Director Karen Self
Design Director Philip Ormerod
Publishing Director Jonathan Metcalf

First published in Great Britain in 2009.
This edition in 2021 by Dorling Kindersley Limited,
DK, One Embassy Gardens, 8 Viaduct Gardens, London, SW11 7BW

The authorised representative in the EEA is Dorling Kindersley
Verlag GmbH. Arnulfstr. 124, 80636 Munich, Germany

Copyright © 2009, 2015, 2021 Dorling Kindersley Limited,
A Penguin Random House Company
10 9 8 7 6 5 4 3 2
002-323121-Dec/21

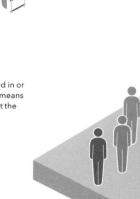

A CIP catalogue record for this book
is available from the British Library.
ISBN: 978-0-2414-8740-2

Printed in China

For the curious
www.dk.com

This book was made with Forest
Stewardship Council ™ certified paper—
one small step in DK's commitment
to a sustainable future. For more
information, go to www.dk.com/our-
green-pledge

Contents

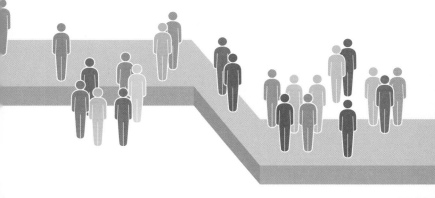

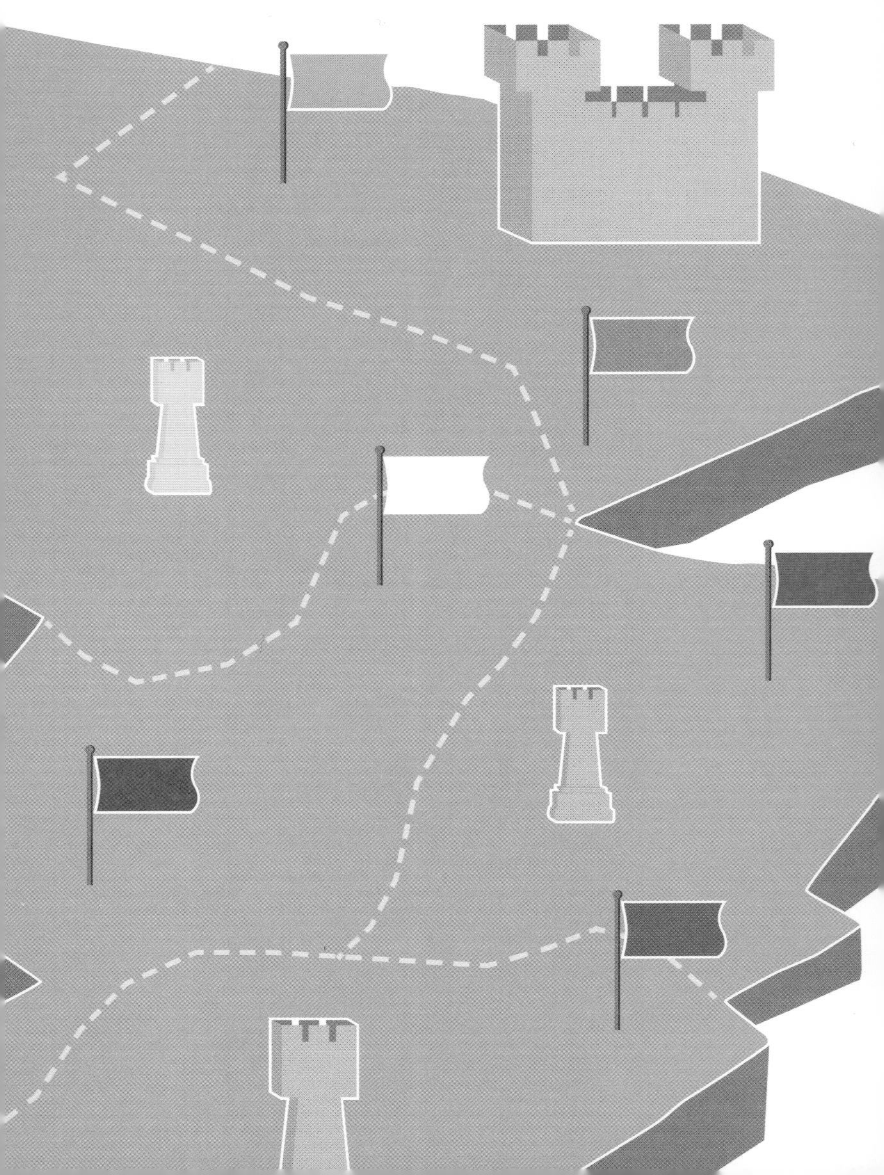

Introduction

Managing other people is perhaps the most challenging task facing any manager. It is a dynamic process that is always evolving to accommodate changes in the diverse and complex workplace. **Managing People** provides the understanding and skills that will help you to develop and create motivated teams, exercising inspirational, supportive, and empathetic leadership.

Being an effective people manager starts with self-awareness and self-management. Interpersonal skills are extremely important, in both one-on-one and team situations, as you need to be able to influence others to accomplish their own and the organization's goals. Building teams who create value for your organization is crucial for any manager today and requires the abilities to set goals, plan and design work, delegate tasks, motivate and coach followers, appraise performance, and solve problems. Today's more fluid work environments mean you'll not only have to know how to exercise these skills in person, but when you and your team are working remotely and flexibly, too.

As a leader of your team, you need to invest considerable time in helping others to create value and develop their careers. Successful mentoring can contribute to fulfilment of personal, professional, and organizational goals. In helping others to be successful by applying the skills and guidelines presented in **Managing People**, you will not only enhance your effectiveness as a manager, but become a leader who others want to follow.

Understanding
yourself

Knowing yourself will give you valuable insights into your aptitude for managing others. It allows you to understand how you are perceived, why people respond to you in the way they do, and how to get the best out of them.

01

Developing self-awareness

Awareness of your emotions, personality, what you enjoy and dislike, what motivates you, and what comes easily or poses challenges is a key precursor to developing effective managerial ability. Quite simply, if you can't manage yourself, you will not be able to manage anyone else.

Keeping moving

The best way to enhance your self-awareness is to learn in a systematic way from your own experiences. Start by reflecting on situations in your working life, your actions in response to them, and the outcomes of these events. Schedule a regular time to do this, either at the beginning or end of a workday, when you are not in the thick of the action. Give yourself space to reflect, and make sure you can be alone and uninterrupted for a good 20 minutes or so. Try to gain a better understanding of what happened and think about how you can learn from each situation.

> Take time to **reflect on situations** in your working life, **your actions** in response to them, and **the outcomes** of these events

Analyzing your performance

Assessing your progress towards your goals can help you gain a fuller understanding of your strengths and weaknesses. Whenever you make a key decision or take a key action, write down what you expect will happen. Then, every three or four months, compare the actual results with your expectations. If you practise this method consistently, it will help you discover what you are doing, or failing to do, that deprives you of the full benefits of your strengths, and will demonstrate areas in which you are not particularly competent and cannot perform adequately.

Tip

MAKE NOTES
Use your journal to **"think on paper"** about what you have read about management in this or other books, or **your experiences** in management training programmes.

In focus

FIND FEEDBACK

It is important to find at least one person in your life who will give you honest, gut-level feedback, to help you gain perspective on your experiences and learn from them. This should be someone you trust enough to go to when you have real problems and ask, "Am I off base here? Am I crazy?" This person could be a partner, a mentor, a best friend, a co-worker, a therapist, or a personal coach. Today, many organizations are providing their managers with 360-degree feedback, allowing them to receive insights on their strengths and weaknesses from other members of staff.

Keeping a journal

Keeping a journal is a good way to help you learn from experience. Journals are similar to diaries, but include entries that address critical aspects of your managerial experiences and reflect on interactions with bosses, employees, and team-mates. If you want to solicit feedback, post your journal as an online blog.

Journal entries could describe:

- ✓ A good (or bad) way someone handled a situation

- ✓ A problem in the making

- ✓ The different ways people react to situations

- ✓ Comments about insightful or interesting quotations

- ✓ Anecdotes, news articles, or even humorous cartoons

- ✓ Your thoughts on people in the news, or in books or films

Using emotional intelligence

Emotional intelligence (EI) is the ability to monitor and work with your and others' emotions. It is measured in EQ, which is the emotional equivalent of IQ. Daniel Goleman – author of the bestselling *Emotional Intelligence* – and other writers suggest that a technically proficient manager with a high EQ will be more successful than a manager who has only a high IQ.

Understanding EQ

Your EQ is the measure of your ability to understand and interact with others and becomes more important the more people you deal with. EQ does not measure personality traits or cognitive capacity. Emotional intelligence can be developed over time and can be improved through training and therapy. Those with a high EQ will be better able to control their own emotions, while at the same time using them as a basis for action. Working with emotions, rather than being at the mercy of them, makes individuals more successful in dealing with the demands of the environment around them. They are better able to control impulses and deal with stress, and better at problem solving. All of these qualities help the individual to perform more competently at work.

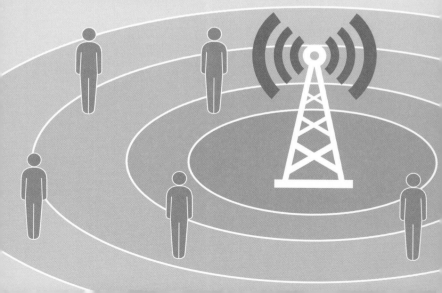

CHECKLIST...
Applying emotional intelligence

		YES	NO
1	Am I **aware of my feelings** and do I act accordingly?	☐	☐
2	Can I **share my feelings** in a straightforward, composed manner?	☐	☐
3	Do I **treat others** with compassion, sensitivity, and kindness?	☐	☐
4	Am I **open to the opinions and ideas** of others?	☐	☐
5	Can I **decisively confront** conflict?	☐	☐
6	Do I **maintain a balance** between my personal life and work?	☐	☐

Using EI at work
To be a successful manager in today's business world, a high EQ may be more important than sheer intellectual or technical ability. A manager who leads a project team of diverse people will need to understand and interact successfully with others. Applying emotional intelligence at work means you are open to the ideas of others and can build and mend relationships with them. You are aware of your feelings and act accordingly, articulating ideas so that others can understand them, developing rapport, building trust, and working towards consensus. Managers who are attuned to their own feelings and the feelings of others use this understanding to enhance personal, team, and organizational performance.

Managing emotions

Emotional intelligence has two aspects: one inward facing and one outward facing. The first of these is your emotional self-awareness and your ability to manage your own emotions. The second is your degree of empathy, or awareness of others' emotions, and your ability to productively manage relationships with others. Both inward- and outward-facing aspects of emotional intelligence are made up of a number of skills or competencies.

The four competencies of emotional intelligence

INWARD COMPETENCIES

SELF-AWARENESS

O Emotional self-awareness

O Accurate self-assessment

O Self-confidence

SELF-MANAGEMENT

O Emotional self-control

O Trustworthiness

O Conscientiousness

O Achievement orientation

O Adaptability

O Optimism

O Initiative

RELATIONSHIP MANAGEMENT
- O **Development of others**
- O **Inspirational leadership**
- O **Influence**
- O **Communication**
- O **Effecting change**
- O **Conflict management**
- O **Bond building**
- O **Teamwork and collaboration**

OUTWARD COMPETENCIES

SOCIAL AWARENESS
- O **Empathy**
- O **Organizational awareness**
- O **Service orientation**

71%
of managers value EQ **more highly** than IQ in their **employees**

Applying assertiveness

An effective manager needs to behave in an active and assertive manner to get things done. Assertive managers are able to express their feelings and act with appropriate degrees of openness and candour, but still have a regard for the feelings or rights of others.

Understanding personality types

Assertiveness and the ability to express feelings are skills that people possess to different extents. Some are aggressive, direct, and blunt, and can appear domineering, pushy, or self-centred. Some people tend to be passive, inhibited, and submissive; they bottle up their feelings and fail even to stand up for their legitimate rights. Passive individuals seek to avoid conflicts and tend to sublimate their own needs and feelings in order to satisfy others.

Assertive behaviour for effective management

Most people fall between the extremes of passive and aggressive. At these extremes, passive and aggressive behaviours hinder effective managerial relations because neither encourages openness. Effective managers need to be assertive, express their ideas and feelings openly, and stand up for their rights, and all in a way that makes it easier for those they are managing to do the same. The assertive manager is straightforward yet sensitive to the

Becoming more assertive

STATE YOUR CASE
Try beginning your conversations with **"I"** phrases, such as **"I think"**, **"I believe"**, or **"I need"**.

BE PREPARED
Prepare for tricky encounters: have all the **facts to hand**, and try to anticipate the other person's replies.

USE OPEN QUESTIONS
If you are finding it hard to get a person to talk to you, use open questions that cannot be answered with a **simple "yes" or "no"** answer.

ASK YOURSELF...

Am I assertive enough?   **YES   NO**

1 Does my response **accurately reflect** how I feel if I'm given a compliment about my work? .... ☐ ☐

2 Am I **able to speak up** when I'm in a group of strangers? .... ☐ ☐

3 If others interrupt me when I am talking, can I **hold my ground**?.. ☐ ☐

4 Do I **avoid being taken advantage of** by other people? .... ☐ ☐

5 Am I able to **criticize others' work** if I think they might react badly? .... ☐ ☐

eeds of others; he or she does not eek to rule over less assertive people. eeking dominance may produce hort-term results but will not make the est use of the team-members' abilities.

> The **assertive** manager is straightforward yet sensitive to the **needs of others**

VISUALIZE YOURSELF

Try assertive role play with a trusted colleague to help you to see yourself as an **assertive person**.

GET PERSPECTIVE

Try to see a situation from the other person's **point of view**. Most workplace bullies, for example, are hiding their own insecurities or an inability to do the job.

BE PATIENT

You'll need **time and practice** to become comfortable with the **new behaviour**. Recognize that those around you may initially be uncomfortable when you start to **become more assertive**.

Examining your assumptions

Managers tend to treat their teams according to assumptions they hold about what motivates people. These assumptions create self-fulfilling prophecies in the behaviour of the team. Managers reward what they expect, and consequently only get what they expect. Challenging your own assumptions is one of the first steps in becoming a better manager.

X-style managers

Prominent management theorist Douglas McGregor distinguished two management styles – X and Y – based on the assumptions held by managers about the motives of their team. X-style managers believe that workers need to be coerced and directed. They tend to be strict and controlling, giving their workers little latitude and punishing poor performance. They use few rewards and typically give only negative feedback. These managers see little point in workers having autonomy, because they think that the workforce neither expects nor desires cooperation.

Y-style managers

Y-style assumptions reflect a much more optimistic view of human nature. Y-style management contends that people will gladly direct themselves towards objectives if their efforts are appropriately rewarded. Managers who hold Y assumptions assume a great deal of confidence in their workers. They are less directive and empower workers, giving them more responsibilities and freedom to accomplish tasks as they deem appropriate.

Shaping the environment

Organizations that are designed based on X-style assumptions are very different to those designed by Y-style managers. For example, because they believe that their workers are motivated to help the organization reach its goals, Y-style managers will decentralize authority and give more control to workers than X-style managers will. A Y-style manager realizes that most people are not resistant to organizational needs by nature, but may have become so as a result of negative experiences. Y-style managers strive to design structures that involve the team members in

Tip

ANALYZE YOURSELF
Honestly review every **decision you make** and every **task you delegate**. In each case, ask yourself what you assumed those involved would think, and how you expected them to behave. Remember that **positive expectations** help to produce positive outcomes.

xecuting their work roles, such as articipative management and joint goal etting. These approaches allow team nembers to exercise some self-direction nd self-control in their work lives.

In Y-style management, although ndividuals and groups are still ccountable for their activities, the role f the manager is not to exert control but to provide support and advice, and to make sure that workers have the resources they need to effectively perform their jobs. By contrast, X-style managers consider their role to be to monitor workers to ensure that they contribute to the production process and do not threaten product quality.

X and Y assumptions

X-STYLE MANAGERS

O Team members inherently dislike work and will attempt to avoid it.

O Workers must be coerced, controlled, or threatened with punishment to achieve goals.

O Team members will shirk responsibility and seek formal direction.

O Most workers place security above all other factors associated with work and will display little ambition.

Y-STYLE MANAGERS

O People can enjoy work and can view it as being as natural to them as rest or play.

O People will exercise self-direction and self-control if they are committed to the objectives behind tasks.

O The average person can learn to accept and seek responsibility.

O Most workers place job satisfaction and career fulfilment high on their list of priorities.

Clarifying your values

Values are stable and enduring beliefs about what is good, right, and worthwhile, and about the behaviour that is desirable for achieving what is worthwhile. To be an effective manager, it is necessary to have a good understanding of what your values are and to act accordingly.

Defining values

Values are formed early in our lives, from the influence of our parents, teachers, friends, religious leaders, and media role-models. Some may change as we go through life and experience different behaviours. Your values manifest themselves in everything you do and the choices that you make. If you are someone who particularly values promptness, for example, you will make sure that you always behave in ways that mean you are on time for appointments. The thought of being late will stimulate feelings of stress in you, and induce a subsequent adrenaline rush as you hurry to be at the appointment on time. As a manager, it is important for you to clarify your values, so that you can determine what your goals are and how you want to manage yourself and others to achieve them.

Clarifying your personal values

It may sound strange, but one of the best ways to clarify your personal values and gain a clear understanding of what is important to you is to think about how you would like to be remembered in your eulogy. Sit quietly and consider how you want your friends and family to remember you, and what you want your work colleagues to

say they thought of you. Also think of your broader contributions – how would you like to be remembered in the communities you are a part of? Make notes, and use the information you write down to identify the values that are most important to you.

Dealing with conflicts

It can be challenging when your personal values conflict with those of your organization, or when there are conflicting values between individuals or sub-groups. Value differences can exist, for example, about how to perform jobs,

ASK YOURSELF...
About your influences   **YES   NO**

1 Can I identify the individuals and the events that
influenced the development of my **value system**? .... ☐ ☐

2 Are these sources of influence **still as important to me**
as recent events and people who influence me now? .... ☐ ☐

3 Are my values **still appropriate** as guides of behaviour
in the world I live in today? .... ☐ ☐

4 Should I consider changing some of my values to make
them **more relevant**? .... ☐ ☐

he nature of reward systems, or the degree of intimacy in work relationships. Having a clear understanding of your own personal value set will help you to manage these conflict situations. If you are clear about your own values, you can act with integrity and practise what you preach regardless of emotional or social pressure. To address a conflict situation, first make sure you are aware of, understand, and are tolerant of the value differences held by the other parties. This will help you to determine whether the value conflict is, in fact, irresolvable and will require personnel changes, or whether compromises and adjustments can be made to accommodate the different perspectives.

In focus

TYPES OF VALUE
Values can be classified into two types: terminal and instrumental. **Terminal values** (your "ends" in life) are desirable ends or goals, such as a comfortable, prosperous life, world peace, great wisdom, or salvation. **Instrumental values** (the "means" to those ends) are beliefs about what behaviours are appropriate in striving for desired goals and ends. Consider a manager who works extra hours to help deliver a customer's rush order. The attitude displayed is a willingness to help a customer with a problem. The value that serves as the foundation of this attitude might be that of service to others.

Developing your personal mission statement

A personal mission statement provides you with the long-term vision and motivation to manage yourself and others in your team according to your own values. It also allows you to establish your purpose and goals as a manager and sets a benchmark for self-evaluation.

Defining your future

Your personal mission statement spells out your managerial philosophy. It defines the type of manager you want to be (your character), what you want to accomplish (your contributions), and what principles guide your behaviour (your values). It provides you with the vision and values to direct your managerial life – the basis for setting long- and short-term goals, and how best to deploy your time.

Setting out your philosophy

Make sure that your personal mission statement is an accurate reflection of your values, goals, and aspirations for

SEE THE FUTURE
Develop a vision of what it will be like when you achieve your goals. Your vision of a desirable future can be **a powerful motivating force**.

EVALUATE PROGRESS
Continually evaluate your performance against your **mission statement**. When things don't work out, be honest with yourself about wh

Tip

LEARN FROM SETBACKS
Things will not always work out as you have planned. When you face setbacks, **be honest with yourself** about what happened and why, and think carefully about whether you need to **re-evaluate your goals**.

success. A personal statement might read: "My career goals are to effectively manage my team to achieve respect and knowledge, to use my talents as a manager to help others, and to play an active role in this organization." Another individual's statement might have a very different focus: "As a manager in this creative firm, I want to establish a fault-free, self-perpetuating learning environment." Re-evaluate your mission statement on a regular basis – annually, at least – to ensure that it still describes your overall vision for your future as a manager

Setting and attaining your personal managerial goals

BE SMART
Set goals that are **Specific**, **Measurable**, **Attainable**, **Realistic**, and **Time-bound** (see pp.50–51). You are more likely to achieve goals that are well defined and within reach.

REWARD YOURSELF
Reward yourself for small wins. When you achieve **incremental progress** towards your goals, treat yourself to a reward, such as a night out or some recreational activity.

GET SUPPORT
Develop a support group of people who will **help you in achieving your goals**. Your support group should include those with the resources you need to be successful.

SET YOUR GOALS
Personalize your goals. You will be **far more committed** to goals that you have set yourself, rather than those that have been set for you by someone else.

Interacting
with others

Your effectiveness as a manager is defined by your ability to interact with other people. A manager needs to guide others through careful communication, teaching, and assessment to work to their full potential, both individually and as a team.

02

Communicating effectively

With flexible working now widespread, investing in communication is more essential than ever. The ability to convey information effectively to those you manage is proven to increase commitment, in turn boosting revenue and the quality of your products or services.

Getting your message across

Communication is the process of sending a message to another person with the intent of evoking an outcome or a change in behaviour. It is more efficient when it uses less time and fewer resources; it is effective when the information is conveyed exactly as you intend. Good communication means balancing the two; for example, explaining a new procedure to each team member individually may be less efficient than calling a meeting where everyone can hear about it. However, if team members have very disparate sets of interests, one-to-one coaching may be more effective.

Delivering messages

Before you send a message, ask yourself how much you **understand about it**, and what is the level of the recipient's understanding

The components of the communication process are the sender, the receiver, the message, and the channel. First, the message is encoded into a format that will get the idea across. Then it is transmitted through the most appropriate channel. This is chosen on the basis of efficiency and effectiveness, as well as practical factors, such as the need to produce a stable record of the communication; whether the information needs to be kept confidential; speed and cost; and the complexity of the communication.

Channels can be oral (speeches, meetings, phone calls, presentations, or informal discussions); written (letters, memoranda, reports, or manuals); electronic (emails, text messages,

Case study

MAKE A PLAN

When Covid-19 hit in 2020, Australian software firm Atlassian, like many organizations, found itself with a raft of changes to communicate to its 6,000 staff members as they switched to homeworking. Its solution was an internal communications plan centred on a 4x7 grid. Four headings across the top identified the **content** of the communications it needed to get out (CEO messages, Covid news...); the **audiences** it needed to get them to (execs, managers, all staff...); the **channels** it would use to do it (live streams, chats, intranet...); and the **purpose** each communication served (keeping leadership visible, providing resources...). Down the side, seven **frequencies** (daily, weekly, monthly etc) marked how often each type of communication needed to go out. By combining such an organized approach with flexibility, openness, and empathy, Atlassian's management was able to provide much-needed consistency and stability at a time of major upheaval.

instant messages, podcasts, video calls, websites, or webcasts); or nonverbal (facial expression, or intonation).

Finally, the message must be successfully decoded by the receiver. Many factors may intrude, preventing the receiver from correctly understanding what they are told. These range from language barriers and semantics to different word interpretations or different frames of reference, cultural attitudes, and mistrust.

Before you send a message, ask yourself how much you understand about it, and what is the level of the recipient's understanding? Will the recipient understand the language and jargon you use, and do they have technology that is compatible with yours?

Tip

COMMUNICATING AT A DISTANCE

Digital communication makes it harder to pick up – and give out – all the **visual cues** that people rely on in person. Whether using video chat, phone call, email, or instant message, **remote managers** need to **talk** more regularly, **listen** more carefully, communicate more **clearly**, and show more **empathy** to team members to ensure effective collaboration.

Sending messages

Effective communication with those you are managing requires that you send clear and comprehensible messages that will be understood as you intend them to be. You can deliver messages more effectively by making them easier to understand and developing your credibility.

Getting your point across

To be successful, all managers must develop the ability to send clear, unambiguous messages that efficiently convey the information they want to deliver. Effective messages use multiple channels to get the information across; for example, if you match your facial and body gestures to the intended meaning of a message while drawing a diagram to explain it, you are using three channels. Make sure that you take responsibility for the feelings and evaluations in your messages, using personal pronouns such as "I" and "mine". Make the information in your messages specific, and refer to concrete details, to avoid the possibility of misinterpretation. Keep your language simple, and avoid technical jargon.

Being credible
Sender credibility is reflected in the recipient's belief that the sender is trustworthy. To increase your sender credibility, ensure that you:

Know what you are talking about: recipients are more attentive when they perceive that senders have expertise.

Establish mutual trust: owning up to your motives can eliminate the recipient's anxiety about your intentions.

Make appropriate self-disclosures: responsibly revealing your feelings, reactions, needs, and desires to others is essential when establishing supportive relationships. It facilitates congruency, builds trust and credibility, and helps recipients of your messages develop empathy and understanding with you.

Be dynamic: being confident, dynamic, and positive in your delivery of information will make you seem more credible than someone who is passive, withdrawn, and unsure.

CHECKLIST...

Communicating using effective messages

		YES	NO
1	Do I use **multiple channels** when sending messages?	☐	☐
2	Do I provide all **relevant information**?	☐	☐
3	Am I **complete and specific**?	☐	☐
4	Do I use "I" statements to **claim my messages** as my own?	☐	☐
5	Am I **congruent** in my verbal and nonverbal messages?	☐	☐
6	Do I use **language** that the receiver can **understand**?	☐	☐
7	Do I **obtain feedback** to ensure that my message has been understood and not misinterpreted?	☐	☐

Share all relevant information: senders are seen as unethical when they intentionally provoke receivers into doing things they would not have done if they had had all of the information.

Be honest: one of the key things people want in a leader and co-worker is honesty. As a sender, avoid any form of deception, which is the conscious alteration of information to influence another's perceptions.

Be warm, friendly, and supportive: this will give you more personal credibility than a posture of hostility, arrogance, or abruptness.

Be reliable: if you are dependable, predictable, and consistent, recipients will perceive you as being trustworthy.

Make information in your messages **specific**, and refer to **concrete details**, to avoid misunderstandings

Listening actively

Many communication problems develop because listening skills are ignored, forgotten, or taken for granted. Active listening is making sense of what you hear. It requires paying attention and interpreting all verbal, visual, and vocal stimuli presented to you.

Understanding the basics

Active listening has four essential ingredients: concentration, empathy, acceptance, and taking responsibility for completely understanding the message. To listen actively, you must concentrate intensely on what the speaker is saying and tune out competing thoughts that create distractions. Try to understand what the speaker wants to communicate rather than what you want to understand. Listen objectively and resist the urge to start evaluating what the person is saying, or you may miss something. Finally, do whatever is necessary to get the full, intended meaning from the speaker's message – listen for feelings and content, ask questions to ensure you have understood.

 Tip

REDUCE NOISE
To use active listening on voice and video chats, be sure to call from a **quiet place**, telling others nearby not to disturb you. On video calls, **mute your mic** when not speaking and **watch the screen** to ensure you're taking everything in.

LISTENING WELL

Dos	Don'ts
O **Keeping an open mind, free from preconceived ideas**	O Judging the value of the speaker's ideas by appearance and delivery
O **Giving the speaker your full attention**	O Thinking about what you are going to say while the speaker is talking
O **Assessing the full meaning behind the words that are being spoken**	O Listening for specific facts rather than the overall message
O **Asking questions when you need more information**	O Interrupting the speaker when you have a better idea
O **Withholding judgement until the speaker has finished talking**	O Always trying to have the last word

Employing the techniques

Active listening is hard work and starts with your own personal motivation. If you are unwilling to exert the effort to hear and understand, no amount of additional advice is going to improve your listening effectiveness. If you are motivated to become an effective listener, there are a number of specific techniques you can use to improve your skills (see below).

Make eye contact: this focuses your attention, reduces the likelihood that you will become distracted, and encourages the speaker.

Show interest: use nonverbal signals, such as head nods, to convey to the speaker that you're listening.

Avoid distracting actions: looking at your watch or shuffling papers are signs that you aren't fully attentive and might be missing part of the message.

Ask questions: seek clarification if you don't understand something. This also reassures speakers that you're listening to them.

Take in the whole picture: interpret feelings and emotions as well as factual content.

Paraphrase: restate what the speaker has said in your own words with phrases such as "What I hear you saying is..." or "Do you mean...?"

Don't interrupt: let speakers complete their thoughts before you try to respond.

Confront your biases: use information about speakers to improve your understanding of what they are saying, but don't let your biases distort the message (see pp.46–47).

Reading nonverbal cues

Nonverbal communication is made up of visual, vocal, and tactile signal and the use of time, space, and image. As much as 93 per cent of the meaning that is transmitted in face-to-face communication can come from nonverbal channels, so you should be aware of these cues.

Decoding the truth

Body language is the visual part of nonverbal communication. It includes expressions, eye movement, posture, and gestures. The face is the best communicator of nonverbal messages. By "reading" a person's facial expression, we can detect unvocalized feelings. Appearance is important, too – people do judge a book by its cover, and most of us react favourably to an expected image. The same goes for posture – a relaxed posture, such as sitting back with legs stretched out and hands behind the head, signals confidence.

Conflicts of meaning

If a person says one thing but communicates something different through intonation and body language, tension and distrust can arise; the receiver will typically choose the nonverbal interpretation because it is more reliable than the verbal. Misunderstandings are more likely to occur during video chats where facial expressions are sometimes the only nonverbal channel available. Aim to include your whole torso in the frame and use arm gestures to convey more information. At the same time, adopt clear, open body language: sit upright, speak confidently, look into the camera, and avoid fiddling or checking your messages – doing so is more obvious than you think.

Posture is important – a **relaxed** posture, such as sitting back with legs stretched out and hands behind the head, **signals confidence**

eelings that can be read from estures and body language

ERVOUSNESS
earing one's throat, **covering** the mouth while peaking, **fidgeting**, **shifting** weight from one ot to the other, **tapping** fingers, **pacing**.

OREDOM OR IMPATIENCE
rumming fingers, foot **swinging**, **brushing picking** at lint, **doodling**, or **looking** at e's phone, watch, or computer screen.

ONFIDENCE, SUPERIORITY, AND AUTHORITY
sing relaxed and expansive gestures, such as **leaning back** ith fingers laced behind the head and hands together at the ack with chin thrust upward.

PENNESS
olding hands in an **open position**, having an **nbuttoned coat** or collar, removing one's coat, **oving closer**, leaning slightly forward, and **ncrossing arms** and legs.

EFENSIVENESS
olding **body rigid**, with arms or legs tightly **crossed**, ves **glancing sideways**, minimal eye contact, lips **ursed**, fists clenched, and a **downcast head**.

Teaching skills

As a manager, an important part of your role is to help those you are managing to develop their skills. If you can encourage the development of skills such as self-awareness, communication, and time management, you will be rewarded with a high-performing team.

Learning by experience

People learn faster and retain more information if they have to exert some kind of active effort. The famous quote, attributed to Confucius: "I hear and I forget. I see and I remember. I do and I understand" is frequently used to support the value of learning through experience. A major implication of this notion is that new skills can be learned only through experimenting with new behaviours, observing the results, and learning from the experience.

Watching, thinking, and doing

The learning of new skills is maximized when learners get the opportunity to combine watching, thinking, and doing. The experiential learning model encompasses four elements: learning new

concepts (conceptualizing), planning how to test the ideas (plan to test), actively applying the skill in a new experience (gaining concrete experience), and examining the consequences of the experience (reflective observation). After reflecting on the experience, learners use the lessons they have learned from what happened to create a refined conceptual map of the skill, and the cycle continues.

To use the experiential learning model to teach skills, you need to: ensure that learners understand the skill both conceptually and behaviourally; give them opportunities to practise it; give feedback on how well they are performing the skill; and encourage them to use the skill often enough so that it becomes integrated into their behavioural repertoire.

> **Tip**
>
> ### LEARN AT A DISTANCE
> Employ the experiential learning model remotely by using online materials (videos, articles, blogs, podcasts, tests, presentations...) – create them yourself or get them from a third party. When working one-to-one or giving feedback, use virtual coaching sessions.

How to teach new skills

01 Help learners to form a **conceptual understanding** of a new skill.

02 Plan how they can **test their understanding** of the skill.

03 Get learners to apply the new skill in **concrete experience**.

04 **Observe what happened** and discuss ways in which they can improve.

Encourage others to **use a skill** often enough so that it becomes **integrated into** their behavioural repertoire

Inspiring others

When you endeavour to teach new skills to others, you are attempting to motivate specific behaviour changes in them. This is more effective if you can convince those you are teaching that, by acting as you suggest, they will gain something that they value. Successful teaching requires you to inspire others to want to cooperat with you. However, different people consider different skills to be more or less valuable to them, so you will also

Effective approaches to teaching skills

APPROACH

BEING PREPARED	**Knowing ahead of time** what you want the outcome of your skills training to be.
LISTENING	Keeping **communication lines open** and indicating to others that **their opinions are important**.
USING QUESTIONS	Presenting a concept, options for applying it, an the consequences, then **asking the learner** wha they will do.
BEING POSITIVE	Correcting mistakes in a **positive way**, not in one that is patronizing or makes others feel worthless and inferior.
BEING HONEST AND UPFRONT	Making it clear to the learner what is **really required of them**, and why this is important.
SETTING PERFORMANCE TARGETS	Indicating the **acceptable level of performance you expect** from those you are teaching, and holding them to it.

…iscover that the majority of responsibility …or the learning of a new skill rests with …he person you are teaching. Learners …ho really want to improve their skills …nd are willing to put in the effort …ill be successful.

Successful teaching requires you to **inspire others** to want to **cooperate** with you

WHY IT WORKS

Unless you know **where you want things to go**, you won't know how to conduct yourself to get there.

The key to **learning a skill effectively** is often expressed by the learner, but overlooked by the manager when they fail to hear it.

Asking rather than telling a team member how best to apply a new skill shows respect, and, because it allows them to **think it through for themselves**, it helps them to learn faster.

Using **positive messages**, such as "I can see that you want to do well and I think that I can help you learn to do better", will help to **motivate** the person you are teaching.

People will be more willing to accept your skill-teaching if they **trust and respect** you for being **honest and forthright**.

In the long run, people will **respect you more** if you hold them to a standard of performance, as they will know any praise they receive from you is **sincere and deserved**.

Giving feedback

Most managers will enthusiastically give their employees positive feedback but often avoid or delay giving negative feedback, or substantially distort it, for fear of provoking a defensive reaction. However, improving employees' performance depends on balanced and considered feedback.

Valuing feedback

Providing regular feedback to your team members will improve their performance. This is because:

- Feedback can induce people to set goals, which act as motivators of their performance.
- Feedback tells people how well they are progressing towards those goals. Positive feedback gives reinforcement, while constructive negative feedback can result in increased effort.
- The content of the feedback will suggest ways that people can improve their performance.
- Providing feedback demonstrates to people that you care about how they are doing.

Feedback should come from a **credible source** and be supported by **hard data**

Dealing with the negative

As a rule, positive feedback is usually accepted readily, while negative feedback often meets resistance. When preparing to deliver negative feedback, first make sure you are aware of any conflict that could arise and think about how to deal with it. Ensure that negative feedback comes from a credible source, that it is objective, and that it is supported by hard data such as quantitative performance indicators and specific examples.

83%

of employees **appreciate** getting **feedback** – whether it's **positive or negative**

GIVE DETAIL

Avoid vague statements such as "I'm impressed with the job you did", or "You have a bad attitude". Recipients need to **understand exactly** what they have or haven't done well.

EXPLAIN YOUR REASONS

Explain to recipients **why you are being critical or complimentary** about specific aspects of their performance.

USE GOALS

Keep feedback **goal-oriented**. Its purpose is not to unload your feelings on someone.

MAKE IT ATTAINABLE

When delivering negative feedback, make sure you only criticize shortcomings over which the person has **some control**.

TALK ABOUT THE JOB

Keep feedback **job-related**. Never make personal judgements, such as "You are stupid and incompetent".

BE NON-JUDGEMENTAL

Keep feedback **descriptive and fair** rather than judgemental.

CHECK UNDERSTANDING

Once you have given your feedback, have recipients rephrase the content to **check that they have fully understood** what you have said and are taking away the right message from your feedback session.

ENSURE A GOOD FIT

Tailor the feedback to fit the person. Consider **past performance** and **future potential** in designing the frequency, amount, and content of performance feedback.

Negotiating

Negotiation is a process by which two or more parties seek to reach agreement about something. Managers spend a lot of time negotiating, and need to be able to do it well. They have to negotiate salaries for incoming employees, cut deals with superiors, bargain over budgets, work out differences with associates, and resolve conflicts between members of their team.

Understanding approaches

There are two general approaches to negotiation: distributive and integrative bargaining. Distributive bargaining assumes zero-sum conditions, that is: "Any gain I make is at your expense", and vice versa. Integrative bargaining assumes a win–win solution is possible. Each is appropriate in different situations.

Distributive bargaining tactics focus on getting an opponent to agree to a deal that meets your specific goals. Such tactics include persuading opponents of the impossibility of getting their needs met in other ways or the advisability of accepting your offer; arguing that your position is fair, while theirs is not; and trying to get the other party to feel emotionally generous towards you and accept an outcome that meets your goals.

> Distributive bargaining tactics focus on getting an opponent to **agree to a deal** that meets your **specific goals**

Finding solutions

Integrative, or win–win, bargaining is generally **preferable** to distributive bargaining.

Case study

A WIN–WIN SOLUTION

After closing a $15,000 order from a small clothing retailer, sales rep Deb Hansen called in the order to her firm's credit department, and was told that the firm could not approve credit for this customer because of a past slow-pay record. The next day, Deb and the firm's credit supervisor met to discuss the problem. Deb did not want to lose the business; neither did the credit supervisor, but he also didn't want to get stuck with a bad debt. The two openly reviewed their options. After considerable discussion, they agreed on a solution: the credit supervisor would approve the sale, but the clothing store's owner would provide a bank guarantee that would assure payment if the bill was not paid within 60 days.

Distributive bargaining leaves one party a loser, and so it tends to build animosities and deepen divisions between people.

For **integrative bargaining** to work, both parties must **openly share all information**, be **sensitive** to each other's needs, **trust** each other, and **remain flexible**.

ntegrative bargaining builds long-term relationships and facilitates **working together n the future**. It bonds negotiators and allows each to leave the bargaining table feeling that e or she has achieved a victory.

Negotiating well

Careful attention to a few key guidelines can increase
a manager's odds of successful negotiation outcomes.
Always start by considering the other party's point
of view. Acquire as much information as you can
about their interests and goals. Always go into
a negotiation with a concrete strategy. Treat
negotiations the way expert players treat the
game of chess, always knowing ahead of time
how they will respond to any given situation.

**How to negotiate
attentively**

Begin with a **positive
overture**, and establish
rapport and mutual
interests.

80%

of a negotiator's efforts
should go into **preparation**
– only around **20%** should
go into **execution**

Make a **small concession**
early on if you can.
Concessions **tend to be
reciprocated** and can lead
to a quick agreement.

Concentrate on the issues,
not on the personal
characteristics or
personality of your
opponent.

Start a negotiation by **considering** the other party's **point of view**

Emphasize **win–win solutions** to the negotiation.

Focus on the **other person's interests** and your own **goals and principles** while you generate other possibilities.

Make your decisions based on **principles** and **results**, not emotions or pressure.

Pay little attention to initial offers, treating them as merely **starting points**.

If any of your opponents attack you or become emotional, **let them blow off steam** and don't take it personally.

Always go into a negotiation with a **concrete strategy** and **knowing** how the other party will **respond** to any given situation

Managing conflict

Conflict is natural within organizations and can never be completely eliminated. If not managed properly, conflict can be dysfunctional and lead to undesirable consequences, such as hostility, lack of cooperation, and even violence. When managed effectively, conflict can stimulate creativity, innovation, and change.

Roots of disagreement

Conflicts exist whenever an action by one party is perceived as preventing or interfering with the goals, needs, or actions of another. Conflicts have varying causes but tend to be rooted in one of three areas: problems in communication; disagreements over work design, policies, and practices; and personal differences.

Understanding the causes

Misunderstandings, semantic difficulties, or poor listening may be the cause of disagreements. Communication breakdowns are inevitable in work settings, often causing workers to focus on placing

25%

of people report that they have **taken time off** to avoid conflict at work

blame on others instead of trying to solve problems. Conflicts can also result when people or groups disagree over goal priorities, decision alternatives, performance criteria, and resource allocations. The things that people want, such as promotions, pay increases, and office space, are scarce resources that must be divided up. Ambiguous rules, regulations, and performance standards can also create conflicts.

Individual idiosyncrasies and differences in personal value systems originating from different cultural backgrounds, education, experience, and training often lead to conflicts. Stereotyping, prejudice, ignorance, and misunderstanding may cause people who are different to be perceived by some to be untrustworthy adversaries.

> **Tip**
>
> ### RESOLVE REMOTELY
> Working remotely means more **written communication**, and so more risk of conflict – overly brief replies, for instance, can mistakenly come across as rude. Encourage staff to **assume the best** of their colleagues, and to **craft** clear messages. In the event of a problem, **switch** to phone or video to better gauge the tone.

Handling conflict

Here are five basic approaches managers can use to try to resolve conflicts. Each has strengths and weaknesses, so choose the one most appropriate to your situation:

Avoidance: not every conflict requires an assertive action. Avoidance works well for trivial conflicts or if emotions are running high and opposing parties need time to cool down.

Accommodation: if you need to maintain a harmonious relationship, you may choose to concede your position on an issue that is much more important to the other party.

- **Competition:** satisfying your own needs at the expense of other parties is appropriate when you need a quick resolution on important issues, or where an unpopular action must be taken.
- **Compromise:** this works well when the parties are equal in power, or when you need a quick solution or a temporary fix to a complex issue.
- **Collaboration:** use this when the interests of all parties are too important to be ignored. Discuss the issues openly and honestly with all parties, listen actively, and carefully deliberate all of the alternatives.

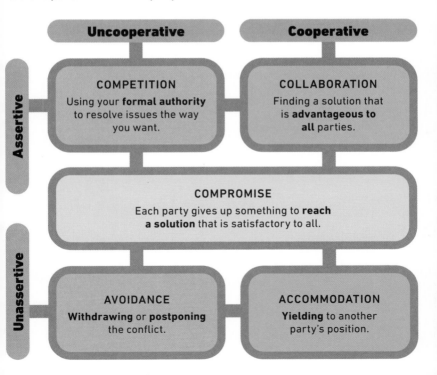

Uncooperative	Cooperative
Assertive	
COMPETITION Using your **formal authority** to resolve issues the way you want.	**COLLABORATION** Finding a solution that is **advantageous to all** parties.
COMPROMISE Each party gives up something to **reach a solution** that is satisfactory to all.	
Unassertive	
AVOIDANCE **Withdrawing** or **postponing** the conflict.	**ACCOMMODATION** **Yielding** to another party's position.

Valuing diversity

Bonding with people at work who are similar can be challenging enough, but bridging the gap and authentically connecting with people who are different demands a specific skill set. As workplaces become more diverse and business becomes more global, managers must understand how cultural diversity affects the expectations and behaviour of everyone in the organization.

Understanding the changes

The labour market is dramatically changing. Most countries are experiencing an increase in the age of their workforce, increased immigration, and, in many, a rapid increase in the number of working women. At the same time, more businesses are selling and manufacturing products and services abroad. As a result, managers must be able to work with people of all backgrounds both inside and outside their organizations, and ensure that their employees can do the same. Workers who believe they are not merely tolerated but valued by their employer are more likely to be loyal, productive, and committed.

> **Tip**
>
> **LET EVERYONE KNOW**
> Make a public commitment to valuing diversity – this will ensure that you are **accountable for your actions**, and may attract potential employees who prefer to work for someone who values **equal opportunities** for all.

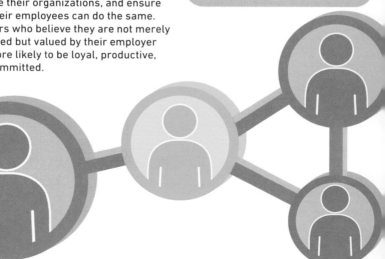

pitalizing on diversity

here's a strong case for boosting
versity and inclusion (D&I). A 2020
tudy by McKinsey & Company showed
at from 2014 to 2019 firms with higher
vels of gender, ethnic, and cultural
versity were more likely to earn higher
rofits than those with lower diversity.
rganizations with more than 30 per cent
male executives outperformed less
ender-diverse ones, while the most
hnically and culturally diverse firms
ere 36 per cent more profitable. D&I
elps organizations avoid "groupthink"
nd to connect with a wider customer
ase. But it's about more than hiring
verse talent. It's how people from
nderrepresented backgrounds feel
bout their workplace that affects if they
ay and advance. Even in diverse firms,
anagers face challenges in creating

equal and open working environments that
instil a sense of belonging. Take these
three steps to boost inclusion:

- Create a level playing field of
  opportunity. Use analytics to show
  that the processes for deciding
  promotions and salaries are
  transparent and fair. Eradicate
  bias from performance reviews.
- Promote a culture that allows people
  to speak up. Discuss issues and
  provide support. Uphold a strict
  anti-discrimination policy, and tackle
  microaggressions.
- Combat bias at the personal level. No
  one is immune from unconscious bias
  and it can shape views on ethnicity,
  religion, age, gender, disability, and
  more. Unconscious bias training can
  raise awareness, better aligning words
  and actions with our conscious values.

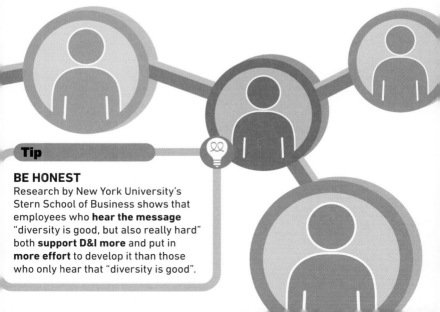

Tip

BE HONEST
Research by New York University's
Stern School of Business shows that
employees who **hear the message**
"diversity is good, but also really hard"
both **support D&I more** and put in
more effort to develop it than those
who only hear that "diversity is good".

Managing
a team

Teams are the cornerstones of many organizations. Successful team leaders understand what makes a team effective and what can lead to failure. To be a successful manager, you need to be able to plan and design the work of your team, delegate tasks effectively, monitor progress, and motivate your team to excel.

03

Setting goals and planning

Planning is a key skill for any manager and starts with having a good understanding of the organization's objectives. It involves establishing a strategy for achieving those goals using the personnel available, and developing the means to integrate and coordinate necessary activities.

Knowing your goals

Planning is concerned with ends (what needs to be done) and means (how those ends are to be achieved). In order to create a plan, managers must first identify the organization's goals – what it is trying to achieve.

Planning and monitoring

Goals are the foundation of all other planning activities. They refer to the desired outcomes for the entire organization, for groups and teams within the organization, and for individuals. In the best organizations, employees and teams work closely with their managers to set their own goals and plan courses of action. Goals provide the direction for all management decisions and form the criteria against which actual accomplishments can be measured.

Tip

LOOK TO THE FUTURE
Write down three SMART goals that you **want your team to achieve** in the next five years, and then **plan how you will reach them**.

How to develop and implement a plan

Define your overall goals, by asking questions such as **"Why do we exist?"** and **"What do we do?"**

Thoroughly analyze your working environment, to **identify opportunities** you can exploit **and threats** you may encounter.

Use the results to **set objectives** that you want to meet. These will create a standard against which to **measure your progress**.

Setting your goals

There are five basic rules that can help you set effective goals. Always make your goals SMART: Specific, Measurable, Aligned, Reachable, and Time-bound.

S **Specific** Goals are meaningful only when they are specific enough to be measured and verified.

M **Measurable** Goals need to have a clear outcome that can be objectively assessed. They also need to have clear benchmarks that can be checked along the way.

A **Aligned** Goals should contribute to the mission, vision, and strategic plan of the organization and be congruent with the values and objectives of the employee implementing them.

R **Reachable** Goals should require you to stretch to reach them, but not be set unrealistically high.

T **Time-bound** Open-ended goals can be neglected because there is no sense of urgency to complete them. Whenever possible, goals should include a time limit.

Goals are the **desired outcomes** for the whole organization, for groups within it, and for individuals

Monitor your progress to **ensure you are on the right track**.

Formulate a plan to achieve those objectives – what needs to be done, by whom, and by when.

Implement the plan, clarifying roles and providing support.

Designing work

Job design refers to the way tasks are combined to form complete jobs. It involves trying to shape the right jobs to conform to the right people, taking into account both the organization's goals and the employees' satisfaction. Well-designed jobs lead to high motivation, high-quality performance, high satisfaction, and low absenteeism and turnover.

Defining jobs

Jobs vary considerably: a lifeguard, for example, will have very different day-to-day responsibilities from an accountant or a builder. However, any job can be described in terms of five core job dimensions:

- **Skill variety:** the degree to which a job requires a variety of different activities so that the worker can employ a number of different skills and talents.
- **Task identity:** the degree to which a job requires completion of a whole and identifiable piece of work.
- **Task significance:** the degree to which a job has an impact on the lives of other people.
- **Autonomy:** the degree to which a job provides freedom and discretion to workers in scheduling their tasks and in determining how the work will be carried out.
- **Feedback:** the degree to which workers get direct and clear information about the effectiveness of their performance.

As a manager, you can maximize your team's performance by enhancing these five dimensions. Skill variety, task identity, and task significance combine to create meaningful work. Jobs with these characteristics will be perceived as important, valuable, and worthwhile.

Jobs that possess autonomy give workers a sense of responsibility for their results. Jobs that provide feedback indicate to the employee how effectively he or she is performing.

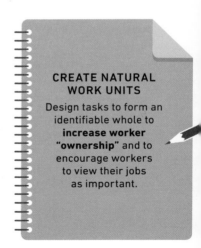

CREATE NATURAL WORK UNITS

Design tasks to form an identifiable whole to **increase worker "ownership"** and to encourage workers to view their jobs as important.

Skill variety, task identity, and task significance combine to **create jobs** that are seen as important, valuable, and worthwhile

COMBINE TASKS

Put existing fragmented tasks together to form larger modules of work. This can help to **increase skill variety** and task identity.

RESPECT DECISIONS

If you have empowered a team member to make a decision, try not to reverse it – unless it really puts the organization in danger. Repeatedly undoing your team members' decisions reduces trust and their sense of autonomy.

Ways to design work by enhancing the five dimensions

EXPAND JOBS VERTICALLY

Giving employees responsibilities formerly reserved for managers closes the gap between the "doing" and "controlling" aspects of the job and **increases autonomy**.

ESTABLISH CLIENT RELATIONSHIPS

Building **direct relationships** between the worker and the client – the user of the product or the service that the employee works on – **increases skill variety**, autonomy, and feedback.

IMPROVE FEEDBACK CHANNELS

Feedback tells team members **how well they are performing**, and whether their performance is improving, deteriorating, or remaining constant. Employees should receive feedback directly as they do their jobs.

High-performing teams

As Lee Iacocca, former CEO of Chrysler Corporation, said: "All business operations can be reduced to three words: people, product, and profit. People come first. Unless you've got a good team, you can't do much with the other two." Successful managers are those who create, work with, and manage successful teams.

Defining high-performing teams

A team is two or more people who meet regularly (whether in person or remotely), perceive themselves as a unit distinguishable from others, have complementary skills, and are committed to a common purpose, a set of performance goals, and an approach for which they hold themselves mutually accountable.

High-performing teams engage in collective work produced by coordinated joint efforts that result in more than the sum of the individual efforts. Research and practical experience have shown that teams with many more than 12 members tend to lack cohesion and struggle to make fast and effective decisions.

Understanding team performance

WHO ARE WE?

Sharing strengths, weaknesses, work preferences, and values allows the establishment of a **set of common beliefs** for the team, creating a group identity and a feeling of **"what we stand for"**.

WHERE ARE WE NOW?

Understanding the current position means that a team can **reinforce its strengths**, improve on its weaknesses, and **identify opportunities** to capitalize on and threats to be aware of.

WHERE ARE WE GOING?

Teams need to have a **vision** of the pot of gold at the end of the rainbow. They also need a **mission**, a **purpose**, and a set of **specific team goals** that they are all excited about.

In focus

MUTUAL TRUST

A climate of mutual trust is essential in a high-performing team – each member of the team needs to know they can depend on the others. Successful managers build mutual trust by creating a climate of openness in which employees are free to discuss problems without fear of retaliation. They are approachable, respectful, and listen to team members' ideas, and develop a reputation for being fair, objective, and impartial in their treatment of others. Consistency and honesty are key, so these managers avoid erratic and unpredictable behaviour and always follow through on any explicit and implied promises they make.

Communication is at the heart of building and maintaining mutual inter-dependence between members of a team. Managers of high-performing teams keep team members informed about upper-management decisions and policies and give accurate feedback on their performance. They are also open and candid about their own problems and limitations.

HOW WILL WE GET THERE?

Team members must understand who will do what and when to **accomplish team goals**, and must be clear about their job description, **roles on the team**, responsibilities, and areas of authority and accountability.

WHAT SUPPORT DO WE GET/NEED?

Reviewing each member's training and development needs can set the stage for **individual training, counselling, and mentoring** that will strengthen both the individual and the team.

HOW EFFECTIVE ARE WE?

Regular performance reviews of quantity and quality outputs and the team process – with recognition and **reward for success** – ensure achievement of team goals and provide members with standards.

Achieving good teamwork

To help your teams perform to the best of their ability, create clear goals. All team members need to have a thorough understanding of the goals of the team and a belief that these goals embody a worthwhile result. This encourages team members to sublimate personal concerns to those of the team. Members need to be committed to the team's goals, know what they are expected to accomplish, and understand how they will work together to achieve these goals.

However, these goals must be attainable; team members can lose morale if it seems that they are not.

To avoid this, set smaller interim milestones in the path to your overall goal. As these smaller goals are attained, your team's success is reinforced. Cohesiveness is increased, morale improves, and confidence builds.

As the manager of a team, it is your job to provide the resources and support that the members need to achieve success. Offer skills training where needed, either personally or by calling in specialists within your organization or outside training services.

Steering your team

Team members should all share in the glory when their team succeeds, but also share the responsibility when the team fails. However, members need to know that they cannot ride on the backs of others.

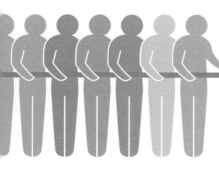

6–12

members is the **ideal number** for a team to work at optimal effectiveness

Identify what each member's contribution to the team's work should be and make it a part of his or her overall performance appraisal. To help monitor performance, select members of the team to act as participant–observers. While a team is working, the role of the participant–observer is to focus on the processes being used – the sequence of actions that takes place between team members to achieve a goal. Periodically, the participant–observer should stop the team from working on its task and discuss the process members are engaged in. The objectives of the participant–observer are to improve the team's functioning by discussing the processes being used and creating strategies for improving them.

CHECKLIST...

Creating a team performance agreement   **YES   NO**

1 Have I identified **what is to be done** and when? .... ☐ ☐

2 Have I **specified the boundaries** (guiding rules of behaviour)
   or the means for accomplishing results? .... ☐ ☐

3 Have I identified the human, financial, technical, or
   organizational support available to help **achieve the results**? ... ☐ ☐

4 Have I established the **standards of performance** and the time
   intervals for evaluation? .... ☐ ☐

5 Have I specified what will happen in **performance evaluations**
   and the consequences of not meeting the standards? .... ☐ ☐

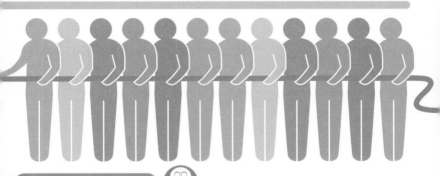

Tip

CHANGE PERSONNEL
If your teams get bogged
down in their own inertia or
internal fighting, **rotate the
members**. Consider how
certain personalities will
mesh and **re-form your
teams** in ways that will
better complement skills.

Setting standards

Create a performance agreement to
record the details of what the team
is aiming to achieve, what is required
and expected of every team member, and
what support will be available to them.
Setting out the framework for team
success clearly helps to ensure that
there is a mutual understanding and
common vision of the desired results
and emphasizes the standards that you
expect from every team member.

Delegating effectively

Managers are responsible for getting things done through other people. You need to accomplish assigned goals by delegating responsibility and authority to others. Empowering others through delegation is one of the most powerful managerial tools for increasing productivity.

Empowering others

Managers delegate by transferring authority and responsibility for work to employees. Delegation empowers employees to achieve goals by allowing them to make their own decisions about how to do a job. Delegation also helps develop employees for promotion opportunities by expanding their knowledge, job capabilities, and decision-making skills.

Delegating lets you **focus on** key **strategic activities** and can also lead to better decision-making

ALLOCATION OF DUTIES
Before a manager can delegate authority, the **tasks** and **activities** that need to be accomplished **must be explained**.

Feeling the benefits

Effective delegation is key for any manager. It will free up your time, allowing you to focus on big-picture strategic activities. It can also lead to better decision-making, because it pushes decisions down the organization, meaning that decision-makers are often closer to the problems. It also helps those you are managing develop their own decision-making skills and prepares them for future promotion opportunities.

The four components of delegation

02

DELEGATION OF AUTHORITY

Delegation is the process of transferring authority to **empower a subordinate** to act for you as a manager.

03

ASSIGNMENT OF RESPONSIBILITY

Managers should assign responsibility to the empowered employee for **performing the job** adequately.

04

CREATION OF ACCOUNTABILITY

Managers should hold empowered employees responsible for properly carrying out their duties. This includes **taking responsibility** for the completion of tasks assigned to them and also **being accountable** to the manager for the satisfactory performance of that work.

Letting go

Managers often have trouble delegating. Some are afraid to give up control, explaining, "I like to do things myself, because then I know they're done right." Others lack confidence in their employees or fear that they may be criticized for others' mistakes. While you may be capable of doing the tasks you delegate better, faster, or with fewer mistakes, it is not possible to do everything yourself. If you often feel that your team isn't taking ownership of projects, it may suggest that you are handing out tasks, rather than delegating responsibility. When you delegate, you should expect, and accept, some mistakes by those you delegate to.

Mistakes are often good learning experiences. You should also put in place adequate mechanisms for feedback so you will know what is happening.

If you do have to intervene, do it with care. While the right help at the right time can be crucial, micromanaging erodes trust. Wait for problems to

How to delegate

CLARIFY THE ASSIGNMENT

Explain **what is being delegated**, the **results** you expect, and the **timeframe**.

SET BOUNDARIES

Ensure that the delegatees **understand precisely** what the parameters are of the **authority** you are bestowing on them.

ENCOURAGE PARTICIPATION

Involve delegatees in **decisions** about what is delegated, how much authority is needed, and **standards** to be attained.

emerge before offering assistance – people are more likely to be receptive to advice once they understand the task themselves. Make it clear that you are there only to help, not to take over, and tailor your approach to fit. Does the situation better suit an intensive burst of help or a series of interventions over a longer term?

20%

of your activity yields **80% of your results**; try to do more of the 20% and delegate the 80%

INFORM OTHERS

Let everyone who may be affected know **what has been delegated to whom** and how much authority has been granted.

ENCOURAGE DEVELOPMENT

Insist from the beginning that when delegatees come to you with a **problem**, they also bring a possible **solution**.

ESTABLISH CONTROLS

Agree on a specific time for **completion of the task**, and set dates when **progress** will be checked and problems discussed.

Motivating others

Every day, people make decisions about how much effort to put into their work. Managers have many opportunities to influence these decisions and motivate their team by providing challenging work, recognizing outstanding performance, allowing participation in decisions that affect employees, and showing concern for personal issues.

Understanding needs

As a manager, you need to understand what drives your team to do the best that they can. American psychologist Abraham Maslow proposed that each person has a five-level hierarchy of needs that they are driven to attempt to satisfy. Once a lower-level need has been largely satisfied, its impact on behaviour diminishes, and the person may need to be motivated to gain the next highest level

There are two aspects to what makes a person perform well: ability and motivation. Ability is the product of aptitude, training, and resources, while motivation is the product of desire and commitment. All of these elements are required for high performance levels.

Maslow's hierarchy of needs

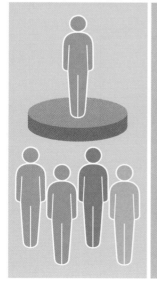

01 ▶▶

PHYSIOLOGICAL NEEDS

Our most basic needs are for **physical survival**, such as to satisfy hunger or thirst. At work, this is receiving enough pay to buy food and clothing and pay the rent.

02 ▶▶

SAFETY NEEDS

Once physiological needs are satisfied, safety needs are aroused. These can be satisfied at work by having **job security** and **safe working conditions**, and receiving **other benefits**.

40%

of UK employees say a **feeling of satisfaction** would **motivate** them more than their **basic salary**

someone is not performing well, the st question you should ask yourself "Is this person's poor performance e result of a lack of ability or a lack motivation?" Motivational methods n often be very effective for proving performance, but if the oblem is lack of ability, no amount of essure or encouragement will help. hat the person needs is training, ditional resources, or a different job.

If you have team members working remotely, keeping them engaged can require extra effort. Remote workers may easily become isolated and lose motivation, so schedule regular video chats to hear their views, gauge their engagement, offer support, and build trust. Also take time to reward their contributions (see pp.64–65) – good work by remote employees can often go unnoticed, draining enthusiasm.

03 ▶▶

SOCIAL NEEDS

Once you feel reasonably secure, social needs begin to take over. At work, this means having **good relationships** with co-workers and participating in company social functions.

04 ▶▶

ESTEEM NEEDS

Next, we are motivated by the need for self-esteem and esteem from others, such as **recognition** for accomplishments and **promotion**.

05 ▶▶

SELF-ACTUALIZATION NEEDS

The highest level is to feel that we are achieving life goals. At work, this means being able to **exercise creativity** and to develop and fully **utilize our skills**.

Using positive reinforcement

Rewarding progress and success and recognizing achievements are powerful ways to motivate your team. By rewarding someone for doing something right, you positively reinforce that behaviour, providing an incentive for doing it again. There are two basic types of reward: extrinsic and intrinsic. Many people depend on and highly value extrinsic rewards that are externally bestowed, such as praise, a promotion, or a pay rise. Others place a high value on intrinsic rewards, which originate from their own personal feelings about how they performed or the satisfaction that they derive from a job well done.

Many depend on **extrinsic rewards** that are externally bestowed, such as praise, promotion, or a pay rise

Case study

PRIORITIZING NEEDS

Theresa, a successful technical writer and a single parent, had been earning a good salary and benefits that enabled her to provide for her family's physical wellbeing: ample food, comfortable housing, and quality clothing. Her company then announced that it was downsizing, and she feared being made redundant. This triggered concerns about her safety needs and meant that she became much less concerned about the higher order needs of belonging to a group or her own self-esteem to perform creative and technically accurate work. Rather, she was motivated to do whatever was necessary to ensure that she kept her job or could find a new one. Once Theresa knew that her job was safe, she changed back to having a higher-order need, energizing her behaviour.

ASK YOURSELF...

Can I draw on my experience?   **YES   NO**

1 Can you think of a coach, teacher, or manager who motivated
you to **enhance your performance** in a particular task? .... ☐   ☐

2 Can you **pinpoint** what this person did to motivate you? .... ☐   ☐

3 Can you remember **how you felt** as a result? .... ☐   ☐

4 Can you **recreate these actions** or use the same approach
when trying to motivate your team?... ☐   ☐

Rewarding success

Try to understand whether each individual
you are managing values intrinsic or
extrinsic rewards more highly. If you
always praise achievements, for example,
a motivated person who excels largely for
the feelings of intrinsic satisfaction will
probably begin to view you as superficial.
The professional may think, "I know I did
a superb job on this project. Why is my
manager being so condescending?"

People also desire different types of
extrinsic rewards. Praise may be perfectly
acceptable to the person motivated by
affiliation and relationship needs, but
may do nothing for the person expecting
a more tangible reward, like money.
Typical extrinsic rewards are favourable
assignments, trips to desirable destinations,
funding for training/education, pay rises,
bonuses, promotions, and office placements.

Motivating your team

STRENGTHENING EFFORT–PERFORMANCE –REWARD EXPECTANCIES

To get the best from your team, emphasize the **anticipated reward value**, whether extrinsic or intrinsic. Make sure that every individual realizes the **link between their performance and the rewards**. Even if your organization does not provide performance-based pay, you can bestow other extrinsic rewards, such as allocating more favourable job assignments.

GIVING PERFORMANCE FEEDBACK

Provide feedback to demonstrate that you know what the members of your team are doing and to **acknowledge improved performance** or a job well done. Especially when individuals are unsure of themselves, you should point out ways in which the person is improving. **Praising specific accomplishments** will help to bolster that person's self-esteem.

CHECKLIST...
Motivating my team

		YES	NO
1	Do I **set clear goals** and **reward success**?	☐	☐
2	Am I **positively reinforcing** successful behaviour?	☐	☐
3	Are the rewards I give **salient to each individual** I am managing?	☐	☐
4	Have I considered **linking pay to performance**?	☐	☐
5	Have I redesigned jobs to **help motivate** the people doing them?	☐	☐
6	Do I make **opportunities to learn** available to my team?	☐	☐

EMPOWERING EMPLOYEES TO ACHIEVE

Empowering the people you are managing, by giving them the **authority**, **information**, and **tools** they need to do their jobs with greater autonomy, can greatly improve their motivation levels.

PROVIDING SALIENT REWARDS

Employees don't all value the same rewards equally, so try to **tailor your rewards** to get the most out of each individual.

REINFORCING THE RIGHT BEHAVIOUR

Quite often what managers say they want, what they reward, and what they get from their team are quite different. If you verbally espouse innovation but reward doing things by the book, you are sending mixed signals and reinforcing the wrong behaviour. **Think carefully about your rewards** and what they mean, and make sure that you reinforce behaviour that you want to see repeated.

Appraising performance

As a manager, you must ensure that objectives are met and also that team members learn how to enhance their performance. Providing feedback through formal performance appraisals can increase productivity and morale, and decrease absenteeism and staff turnover.

Assessing progress

Giving feedback formally in performance appraisal interviews enables you to set goals and monitor achievement, helping to motivate your team. Appraisals allow you to tell how each member is progressing, which can reinforce good behaviour and extinguish bad. But the interview itself is the final step. Appraisal should be a continuous process that starts with establishing and communicating performance standards. Assess how each individual is performing relative to these standards, and then

> Keep your appraisal **goal-oriented**, make sure your feedback is **specific**, and encourage **self-evaluation**

CONDUCTING APPRAISAL INTERVIEWS

Dos	Don'ts
O **Focusing only on feedback that relates to the person's job**	O Sharing your feelings about a person's personality
O **Providing both positive and negative feedback**	O Focusing your comments only on bad performance
O **Sharing first-hand observations as evidence**	O Including rumours and allegations in your appraisal
O **Being unafraid to criticize the person constructively**	O Avoiding offending the other person by sugarcoating your criticism

ASK YOURSELF...

Am I prepared for the appraisal?

	YES	NO

1 Have I **carefully considered** the person's strengths as well as their weaknesses? ☐ ☐

2 **Can I substantiate**, with specific examples, all points of praise and criticism? ☐ ☐

3 Have I **thought about any problems** that may occur in the appraisal interview? ☐ ☐

4 Have I **considered how I will react** to these problems? ☐ ☐

...iscuss this in the interview. Take steps to ...mit unconscious bias in the process and ...nsure all employees are judged equally ...y outlining the competences valued in ...ach role and obliging appraisers to give ...vidence to justify their conclusions.

The appraisal interview

...tart by putting the person at ease. ...ost people don't like to hear their ...ork criticized, so be supportive and ...nderstanding and create a constructive ...limate. If you are conducting the ...terview remotely, there's greater ...oom for miscommunication, so take ...xtra care to talk clearly, listen, and ...e receptive. Begin the interview by ...xplaining what will transpire during ...e appraisal and why. Stay goal-oriented, and make sure your feedback is specific. Where you can, get the person's own perceptions of the problems being addressed – there may be contributing factors you are unaware of. Encourage self-evaluation; people may acknowledge performance problems independently, thus eliminating your need to raise them. They may also offer viable solutions.

Setting action points

At the end of the interview, ask the recipient to rephrase the content of your appraisal. This will indicate if you have communicated your evaluation clearly. Finish by drawing up a step-by-step plan for improvement. Include what needs to be done, by when, and how you will monitor the person's activities.

Leading
others

Leadership is the process of providing direction, influencing and energizing others, and obtaining follower commitment to shared organizational goals. Managers need to lead their team, setting ethical boundaries for them to follow, developing a power base for influencing them to change in positive ways, and helping them improve through coaching and mentoring.

04

Taking an ethical path

Few of us would steal or cheat, but how principled would you be, or should you be, when faced with routine business situations involving ethical choices? As a leader, you need to have a clear understanding of your ethical principles and set a consistent example for your team.

Understanding ethics

Ethics refer to the principles that define good or poor conduct. In the workplace, acting ethically is not just a fanciful idea, it is an everyday occurrence. Consider this dilemma: an employee whose work has been substandard for some time has found another job. You are relieved, but then he asks for a recommendation letter. Do you say no and run the risk that he will not leave? Or do you write it, knowing you are influencing someone else to hire him?

Being responsible

Ethics is important for everyone in an organization, particularly as some unethical acts are also illegal.

Many organizations want employees to behave ethically because such a reputation is good for business, which in turn can mean larger profits. Many employees also want their organizations to behave ethically, citing sustainability and social purpose as increasingly important factors in deciding where to work. Acting ethically is especially crucial for managers. The decisions a manager makes set the standard for those they are managing and help create a tone for the organization. If employees believe all are held to high standards, they are likely to feel better about themselves, their colleagues, and their organization.

ASK YOURSELF...
Is what I'm about to do ethical?   **YES   NO**

1   **Am I clear** why I'm doing what I'm about to do?............................ ☐ ☐

2   Have I acknowledged my **true intentions** in taking this action?.... ☐ ☐

3   Are there any **ulterior motives** behind my action, such
    as proving myself to my peers or superiors?.................................. ☐ ☐

4   Will my actions **injure someone**, physically or emotionally?......... ☐ ☐

5   Would I **disclose** to my boss or my family what I plan to do?.......... ☐ ☐

Organizations want employees to **behave ethically** as having such a reputation is good for business, which in turn can mean **larger profits**

Developing ethics

The behaviour of managers is under more scrutiny than that of other members of staff, and misdeeds can become quickly and widely known, destroying the reputation of the organization. It is important for managers to develop their own ethical boundaries – lines that they and their employees should not cross. To do this, you need to:

O **Know** and **understand** your organization's **policy** on ethics.

O Anticipate unethical conduct. **Be alert** to situations that may promote unethical behaviour. (Under unusual circumstances, even a normally ethical person may be tempted to act out of character.)

O **Consider all consequences**. Ask yourself questions such as: "What if my actions were described in detail on a local TV news show, or social media? What if I get caught doing something unethical? Am I prepared to deal with the consequences?"

O **Seek opinions** from others. They may have been in a similar situation, or at least can listen and be a sounding board for you.

O Do what you truly believe is right. You have a conscience and are responsible for your behaviour. You need **to be true to your own internal ethical standards**. Ask yourself the simple question: "Can I live with what I have decided to do?"

Ensuring cultural fit

An organization's culture, or personality, refers to the key characteristics that it values and that distinguish it from other organizations. Managers need to be aware of organizational culture because they are expected both to respond to its principles themselves, and to develop an understanding of it in those they are managing.

Analyzing organizational culture

The cultural imperatives of an organization are often not written down or even discussed, but all successful managers must learn what to do and what not to do in their organizations. In fact, the better the match between the manager's personal style and the organization's culture, the more successful the manager is likely to be. Founders create culture in three ways. First, they hire and keep employees who think and feel the way they do. Second, founders indoctrinate and socialize these employees to their way of thinking. Third, founders act as role models, and their personality becomes central to the culture of the organization.

Discerning the culture

Many organizations have given little thought to their culture and do not readily display it. To try to find out more about your organization's culture, you might:

- Observe the surroundings. Look at signs, pictures, dress codes, the degree of openness in offices, and how they are furnished and arranged. Also consider how the firm presents itself on its intranet.
- Listen to the language. For example, do managers use military terms, such as "take no prisoners"? Or do they speak about "intuition", "care", and "our family of customers"?
- Ask different people the same question and compare the answers. How does this firm define success? For what are staff most rewarded? Who is on the fast track and what did they do to get there? Are you happy with your work-life balance?

77%

of people would **consider** a company's **culture** before **applying** for a job there

Case study

KEEPING CULTURE CONSISTENT

At coffee retailer Starbucks, all employees go through a set of formal classes during their first few weeks on the job. They are taught the history of the firm, coffee-making techniques, and given coffee-tasting classes. They even receive emotional intelligence training to help them to deliver better customer service. The firm's socialization programme turns out employees who are well versed in the company's culture and can represent Starbucks' obsession with "elevating the coffee experience" for its customers.

Sustaining culture

Managers are responsible for sustaining organizational culture by helping new employees to learn and adapt. (They may also help hire talent, though this is usually a specialist HR task.) A new worker, for example, must be taught what behaviours are valued by the organization, so that they can learn the "system" and assume the behaviours appropriate to their role.

The better the match between your **personal style** as a manager and the **organization's culture**, the more **successful** you are likely to be

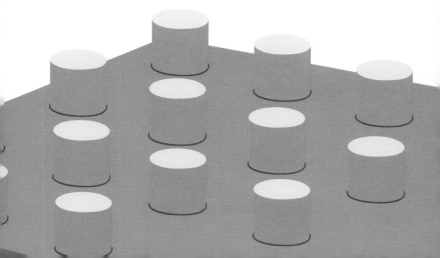

Solving problems

Managerial success depends on making the right decisions at the right times. But unless you define a problem and identify its root causes, it is impossible to make appropriate decisions about how to solve it. Effective managers know how to gather and evaluate information that clarifies a problem, develop alternatives, and weigh up the implications of a plan before implementing it. They are able to analyze data and use their teams to develop creative solutions.

Spotting problems

A problem exists when a situation is not what is needed or desired. A major responsibility for all managers is to maintain a constant lookout for existing or potential problems, and to spot them early before they escalate into serious situations – including grievances that have to be dealt with by HR. Managers fulfil this responsibility by keeping channels of communication open, monitoring employees' current performance, and examining deviations from present plans. Four situations can alert managers to possible problems:

- A deviation from past experience
- A deviation from a set plan
- When other people communicate problems to you
- When competitors start to outperform your team or organization

The problem-solving process

Definition is important even if the **solution to the problem** appears to be obvious

01

IDENTIFYING

Being conscious of what is going on around you, so you can spot problems early.

02

DEFINING

Making a careful analysis of the problem to be solved, in order to define it as clearly as possible.

Finding solutions

Problem solving involves closing the gap between what is actually taking place and a desired outcome. Once you have identified a problem that needs to be addressed, start by analyzing the problem and defining it as clearly as you can. This is a key step: the definition you generate will have a major impact on all remaining steps in the process. If you get the definition wrong, all remaining steps will be distorted, because you will base them on insufficient or erroneous information. Definition is important even if the solution to the problem appears to be obvious – without a full assessment you may miss an alternative resolution that more advantageous.

Gather as much information about the situation as you can. Try to understand the goals of all of the parties involved, and clarify any aspects of the problem you are unclear about.

Developing an action plan

Once you are satisfied that you have a full understanding of the issues, develop courses of action that could provide a resolution to the problem. There is often more than one way to solve a problem, so it is critical to consider all possible solutions and arrive at several alternatives from which to choose.

Implementing and monitoring

Your decision will provide you with an action plan. However, this will be of little value unless it is implemented effectively. Defining how, when, and by whom the action plan is to be implemented and communicating this to those involved is what connects the decision with reality.

Your involvement should not end at implementation. Establish criteria for measuring success, then track progress and take corrective actions when necessary. Try to develop and maintain positive attitudes in everyone involved.

03

MAKING THE DECISION

Evaluating the alternatives and choosing a course of action that will improve the situation in a significant way.

04

IMPLEMENTING

Setting your action plan in motion, by creating a schedule and assigning tasks and responsibilities.

05

FOLLOWING UP

Monitoring progress, to ensure that the desired outcome is achieved.

Building power

Research shows that power is most effective when exercised by those concerned with the interests and needs of others. Learning how to wield your power using social intelligence will help you influence people and develop your career.

Developing power bases

Managerial positions come with the authority to issue directives and allocate rewards and punishments – for example, to assign favourable or unfavourable work tasks, hold performance reviews, and make salary adjustments. But management experts such as Dacher Keltner, author of *The Power Paradox*, argue that true power requires empathy and humility, not forcing or manipulating others into doing your will.

Social intelligence Studies show that socially engaged managers who treat team members with consideration share power, and create a sense of togetherness win and maintain status.

Modesty Research by University of California, Berkeley professors Dacher Keltner and Cameron Anderson found that modest people were more likely to attain and maintain high status and win respect, while those with inflated egos tended to lose respect.

85%

of midsize firms say it's now more important for managers to **show empathy** than before Covid-19

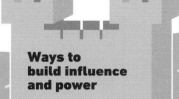

Ways to build influence and power

Being human Artificial Intelligence is taking on many organizational tasks carried out by managers, so emotional intelligence, flexibility, and other more "human" skills are increasingly highly valued and will help boost your status.

Empathy Collectively, we give power to those who serve the interests of the group. Listen and use empathy to see things from the perspective of others so you know how best to collaborate.

Win-win outcomes Research repeatedly shows that it's not manipulative Machiavellian types who rise to power, but individuals who can best understand and advance the interests of others. Power lies with those who can resolve conflicts and mediate tensions in the group.

Impression management A socially intelligent use of power brings measurable returns, including happier employees who perform better. In turn this favourably influences how others see, talk about, and evaluate you.

Types of power

Your power within an organization comes from various sources. Use these different types of power in their correct contexts to maximize your effectiveness as a manager.

Ways to use managerial power to obtain desired outcomes

- **Legitimate power** This derives from your position in the organizational hierarchy and is enhanced by a clear chain of command and corporate structure. In "flat" organizations, which emphasize collective leadership and have few levels of management between staff and the board, this form of power will be limited.
- **Coercive power** The threat of sanction confers power, but should be used carefully – when the organization is in difficulty or crisis.
- **Referent power** This type derives from being respected and admired by those you manage, and encouraging them to imitate your style. Here, giving staff responsibility for their actions enhances your power. It works best in small workplaces, where you can foster one-to-one relationships.
- **Reward power** This comes from the ability to provide incentives and rewards, such as praise or promotion, to those you manage.

Legitimate power derives from your position in the organizational **hierarchy**, and is enhanced by a clear **chain of command** and corporate structure

HIGHER AUTHORITY

Gain the support of those above you to back your requests. This is only effective in hierarchical bureaucratic organizations where there is great respect for authority.

BARGAINING

Exchange benefits or favours to negotiate outcomes acceptable to both parties. This works best when organizational culture promotes give-and-take cooperation.

ASSERTIVENESS

Be direct and forceful when indicating what you want from others. This strategy is most effective when the balance of power is clearly in your favour.

SANCTIONS

Use organizationally derived rewards and punishments to obtain desired outcomes. This approach is only for influencing those you manage, and may be seen as manipulative.

FRIENDLINESS

Use flattery, create goodwill, act humbly, and be supportive prior to making a request. This works best when you are well liked.

COALITIONS

Develop support in the organization for what you want to happen. This is most effective where final decisions rely on the quantity not the quality of support.

REASONING

Use facts and data to make a logical or rational presentation of ideas. This is most effective when others are trustworthy, open, and logical.

Managing change

Individuals, managers, teams, and organizations that do not adapt to change in timely ways are unlikely to survive in our increasingly turbulent world environment. Managers who anticipate change, learn to adapt to change, and respond flexibly will be the most successful.

Overcoming resistance

Change is the process of moving from a present state to a more desired state in response to internal and external factors. To successfully implement change, you need to possess the skills to convince others of the need for change, identify gaps between the current situation and desired conditions, and create visions for desirable outcomes.

Experienced managers are aware that efforts to change often face resistance. This can be for a variety of reasons, including fear, vested interests, misunderstanding, lack of trust, differing perceptions of a situation, and limited resources. You need to be able to counter this resistance to change through education, participation, and negotiation.

Promoting change

Major change does not happen easily. Effective managers can establish a sense of urgency that the change is needed. If an organization is facing a threat to its survival, this usually gets people's attention. Dramatically declining profits and stock prices are examples, as is the 2020 Covid-19 pandemic, which forced organizations to rethink working practices, supply chains, and delivery mechanisms overnight. But as the world

Tip

TURN TO THE POSITIVE
Try to **use any resistance** to your proposed change **for your benefit**, by making it a stimulus for dialogue and a deeper, more thoughtful analysis of the alternatives.

djusts to an uncertain, fast-shifting ost-pandemic world, the ability to nplement change in the absence of n obvious crisis is vital for managers. hey need to be able to identify potential roblems by scanning the external nvironment, and find ways to convey e information broadly and dramatically that others understand the need for hange. They also have to develop and rticulate compelling visions and

strategies to which people will aspire and that will guide the change effort. The vision of the end result should illuminate core principles and values that pull followers together. Lastly, institutionalizing change in the organizational culture refreezes it. New values become instilled in the culture and employees view the changes as normal and integral to operations.

In focus

PHASES OF CHANGE
Planned change progresses through three phases:
Unfreezing This involves helping people see that a change is needed because the existing situation is undesirable. Existing attitudes and behaviours need to be altered during this phase to reduce resistance, by explaining how the change can help increase productivity, for example. Your goal in this phase is to help the participants see the need for change and to increase their willingness to make the change a success.

Changing This involves making the actual change and requires you to help participants let go of old ways of doing things and develop new ones.
Refreezing The final phase involves reinforcing the changes made so that the new ways of behaving become stabilized. If people perceive the change to be working in their favour, positive results will serve as reinforcement, but if not, it may be necessary to use external reinforcements, which can be positive or negative.

Helping others to improve

Helping employees become more competent is an important part of any manager's job. It contributes to a three-way win for the organization, the manager, and the employees themselves. By helping others resolve personal problems and develop skill competencies – and so help them improve their performance – you will motivate your team to achieve better results for themselves and for the organization.

Diagnosing problems

If you can reduce unsatisfactory performance in the people you are managing, you ultimately make your job easier because you will be increasingly able to delegate responsibilities to them. Unsatisfactory performance often has multiple causes. Some causes are within the control of the person experiencing the difficulties, while others are not.

67%

of global employees are not **engaged** with their work, while **18%** are **actively disengaged**

Ways to help others improve

Accept mistakes and use them as **learning opportunities**.

Help **develop action plans** for improvement.

Actively listen to employees and show **genuine interest**.

Recognize and reward even small improvements.

CHECKLIST...

Determining the cause of unsatisfactory performance   **YES** **NO**

1 Is the person **unaware** that his or her performance
is unsatisfactory? If yes, provide feedback .... ☐ ☐

2 Is the person performing poorly through a lack of awareness
of **what is expected**? If yes, provide clear expectations .... ☐ ☐

3 Is performance hampered by obstacles **beyond the person's
control**? If yes, determine how to remove the obstacles .... ☐ ☐

4 Is the person struggling with not knowing how to **perform
a key task**? If yes, provide coaching or training .... ☐ ☐

5 Is **good performance** followed by negative consequences?
If yes, determine how to eliminate the negative consequences .. ☐ ☐

6 Is poor performance rewarded by **positive consequences**?
If yes, determine how to eliminate the positive reinforcement ... ☐ ☐

Seek to **educate** rather than to assist.	Provide **meaningful feedback** for learning.	Encourage continual **improvement**.
Model the **behaviours** you desire.	Demonstrate **unconditional positive regard** by suspending judgement and evaluation.	Ask questions to **help discover** sources of problems.

Demonstrating positive regard

The relationship between you and the person you are helping is critical to the success of the coaching, mentoring, or counselling you undertake with them. For a helping relationship to be successful it is important to hold the person being helped in "unconditional positive regard". This means that you accept and exhibit warm regard for the person needing help as a person of unconditional self-worth – a person of value no matter what the conditions, problems, or feelings. If you can communicate positive regard, it provides a climate of warmth and safety because the person feels liked and prized as a person. This is a necessary condition for developing the trust that is crucial in a helping relationship.

> The person being helped should be held in "unconditional **positive regard**"

Conducting a helping session

Before you speak to someone about how to help them improve their performance, make sure you have **acquired all the facts** about the situation.

Take time to think about **what type of help** the situation requires; consider how the person might react and how they might feel about what you are going to discuss.

Start by discussing the purpose of the **helping session**.

Try to make the person feel **comfortable** and at **ease**.

Establish a **non-defensive** climate, characterized by **open communication** and **trust**.

Before you discuss the problem you have identified, raise and discuss **positive aspects** of the person's performance.

Make sure **expectations** are **clearly understood**.

Mutually define the problem (performance or attitude).

Summarize what has been agreed upon.

Help the other person **establish an action plan** that includes **specific goals** and dates.

Affirm your confidence in the person's ability to make needed changes based on his or her **strengths** or past history.

Mutually determine the causes. Do not interpret or psychoanalyze behaviour; instead, **ask questions** such as, "What's causing the lack of motivation you describe?"

After the session, make sure that you **follow up** to see how the person is **progressing**, and modify the action plan if necessary.

Counselling others

Counselling is the discussion of emotional problems in order to resolve them or to help the person better cope. Problems that might require counselling include divorce, serious illness, financial problems, interpersonal conflicts, drug and alcohol abuse, and frustration over a lack of career progress. Although most managers are not qualified as psychologists, there are several things managers can do in a counselling role before referring someone to a professional therapist.

Confidentiality is of paramount importance when counselling others. To open up and share the reasons for many personal problems, people must feel that they can trust you and that there is no threat to their self-esteem or their reputation with others. Emphasize that you will treat in confidence everything that the other person says regarding personal matters.

In focus

FIRST-RATE FEEDBACK

People need feedback about the consequences of their actions if they are to learn what works and what doesn't and then change their actions to become more effective. Carefully thought-out feedback can increase performance and positive personal development. Applying feedback in the helping process involves:

- Describing observed behaviours and the results and consequences of those behaviours.

- Assessing the impact of the observed behaviours in terms of organizational vision and goals.
- Predicting the personal consequences for the person involved if no changes take place.
- Recommending changes the person could make to improve their behaviour.

This sequence of actions applies whether the type of help being given to the person is coaching, mentoring, or counselling.

92%

of employees agree that "negative feedback, if appropriately delivered, is **highly effective** at **improving performance**"

Confidentiality is paramount when **counselling others**: people must feel that they can trust you

Tip

BE SUPPORTIVE
Reassure those you are counselling that their **problems have solutions** and that they have the ability to improve the situation.

Dealing with personal problems

Getting a person to recognize that he or she has a problem is often the first step in helping deal with it. You can then follow up by helping gain insights into feelings and behaviours, and by exploring the available options.

Sometimes people just need a sounding board for releasing tension, which can become a prelude to clarifying the problem, identifying possible solutions, and taking corrective action. Talking things through in a counselling session can help people sort out their feelings into more logical and coherent thoughts.

Above all, be supportive and provide reassurance. People need to know that their problems have solutions. If problems are beyond a person's capability to solve, explain how professional treatment can be obtained, through Employee Assistance Programmes, for example, or wellbeing plans.

Coaching and mentoring

Coaching is the process of helping people improve performance. A coach analyzes performance, provides insight on how to improve, and offers the leadership, motivation, and supportive climate to help achieve that improvement. In mentoring relationships, a more experienced person formally pairs up with a less experienced one to help show them "the ropes" and to provide emotional support and encouragement.

Helping others develop

As a coach, a manager's job is to help members of their team develop skills and improve. This involves providing instruction, guidance, advice, and encouragement. Effective coaches first establish a supportive climate that promotes development. It is particularly important that you remain non-judgemental and understanding throughout the process, try to solve problems jointly, and educate those you are coaching about how to solve their own problems in the future. As you learn more about the person you are coaching, try to determine the sources of any problems you discover, and provide meaningful feedback.

Coaching a process

To coach successfully, you will need to follow these steps:

- Explain and then demonstrate the process
- Observe the person practising the process
- Provide immediate, specific feedback
- Express confidence in the person's ability
- Agree on follow-up actions.

The role of a mentor

The goal of a mentor is to help a less experienced person achieve his or her career goals. Mentors perform as both coaches and counsellors as they guide their less experienced associates towards improved performance. Mentoring can help new organization members gain a better understanding of the organization's goals, culture, and advancement criteria. It can also help them become more politically savvy and avoid potential career traps. As a mentor, try to help others reduce the stress caused by uncertainty about how to do things and deal with challenging assignments. Be a source of comfort when newer, less experienced people just need to let off steam or discuss career dilemmas.

55%

of **global companies** run internal coaching programmes

Three key skills for successful coaching

01
FINDING WAYS TO IMPROVE PERFORMANCE

O Help others improve by observing what they do, asking questions, listening, and crafting unique improvement strategies.

02
INFLUENCING OTHERS TO CHANGE THEIR BEHAVIOUR

O Monitor people's progress and development, and recognize and reward even small improvements.

O Involve others in decision-making processes – this helps to encourage people to be responsive to change.

O Break large, complex projects into series of simpler tasks – this can boost confidence as the simpler tasks are achieved.

O Be a role model for the qualities that you expect from others, such as openness and commitment.

03
CREATING A SUPPORTIVE CLIMATE

O Use active listening, empower others to implement appropriate ideas, and be available for assistance, guidance, and advice.

Managing careers

In today's rapidly changing business landscape, managers need to actively manage their careers and provide career guidance to those they are managing. To determine where and how you can best contribute, you need to know yourself, continually develop yourself, and be able to ascertain when and how to change the work you do.

Charting your own career path

Self-assessment is an ongoing process in career management. Successful careers develop when people are prepared for opportunities because they know their strengths, their methods of work, and their values. Self-directed career management is a process by which individuals guide, direct, and influence the course of their careers.

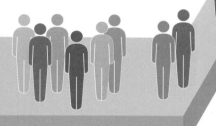

Ensure that those you are **managing** have **reasonable** workloads

This requires exploration and awareness of not only yourself, but also your environment. Individuals who are proactive and collect relevant information about personal needs, values, interests, talents, and lifestyle preferences are more likely to be satisfied and productive when searching for job opportunities, to develop successful career plans, and to be productive in their jobs and careers.

Driving forward

The first step in self-directed career management is planning. Taking your strengths, limitations, and values into account, start searching the environmen for matching opportunities. Use the information you gather to establish realistic career goals and then develop a strategy to achieve them. As you progress through your career plan, regularly undertake performance appraisals to make sure that you are remaining on track and that your goals haven't changed.

Directing others

The most important thing you can do to contribute to the career development of others is to instil in them the need to take responsibility for their own careers. Then you can provide support that will enable

them to add to their skills, abilities, and knowledge, in order to maintain their employability within the organization and avoid obsolescence as a result of technological advances. To help those you are managing develop their careers:

- **Keep your team updated** about the organization's goals and future strategies so that they will know where the organization is headed and be better able to develop a personal career development plan to share in that future.
- **Create growth opportunities** for your team, to give them new, interesting, and professionally challenging work experiences.
- **Offer financial assistance**, such as tuition reimbursement for college courses or skills training.
- **Allow paid time off** from work for off-the-job training, and ensure that those you are managing have reasonable workloads so that they are not precluded from having time to develop new skills, abilities, and knowledge.

In focus

CAREER STAGES
Individuals just beginning their careers are usually more concerned with identifying organizations that have the potential to satisfy their career goals and match their values. After settling into a job, focus shifts to achieving initial successes, gaining credibility, learning to get along with their boss, and managing their image. Managers in the middle of their careers are more concerned with career reappraisal, adding to their skill set, and becoming more of a generalist. In the later stages of their careers, managers focus more on teaching and mentoring others and leaving a contribution before retirement.

Index

Acknowledgments

Stats
p.15 "Seventy-One Percent of Employers Say They Value Emotional Intelligence over IQ, According to CareerBuilder Survey", CareerBuilder, 18 August 2011
p.38 "Employee engagement statistics from across the globe", Officevibe, 25 May 2021
p.42 "Why negotiation is the most popular business school course", Leigh Thompson & Geoffrey J Leonardelli, *Ivey Business Journal*, July / August 2004
p.44 *Workplace Conflict and How Businesses Can Harness It to Thrive: Global Human Capital Report*, CPP, July 2008
p.63 *Living to Work: Employee Motivation Report*, Motivates, 2018
p.74 *Mission & Culture Survey*, Glassdoor, 2019
p.78 "What Does It Mean to Be a Manager Today?", Brian Kropp, Alexia Cambon, & Sara Clark, *Harvard Business Review*, 15 April 2021
p.84 *State of the Global Workplace*, Gallup, 2017
p.89 "Your Employees Want the Negative Feedback You Hate to Give", Jack Zenger & Joseph Folkman, *Harvard Business Review*, 15 January 2014
p.90 *Coaching: A Global Study of Successful Practices – Current Trends and Future Possibilities 2008-2018*, American Management Association, 2008

The publisher would like to thank:
Delhi Team
DTP Designer: Jaypal Singh Chauhan, Mrinmoy Mazumdar
Editor: Saumya Agarwal

Second edition:
Senior Art Editor Gillian Andrews
Project Editor Hugo Wilkinson
Managing Editor Gareth Jones
Senior Managing Art Editor Lee Griffiths
Production Editor Nikoleta Parasaki
Production Controller Mandy Inness
Jacket Designer Mark Cavanagh
Design Development Manager Sophia M.T.T.

Delhi Team:
Senior Editorial Manager Rohan Sinha
Deputy Managing Art Editor Sudakshina Basu

First edition:
Senior Editor Peter Jones
Senior Art Editor Helen Spencer
Production Editor Ben Marcus
Production Controller Hema Gohil
Executive Managing Editor Adèle Hayward
Managing Art Editor Kat Mead
Art Director Peter Luff
Publisher Stephanie Jackson

First and second editions produced for Dorling Kindersley Limited by Cobalt id
www.cobaltid.co.uk

Editor Marek Walisiewicz
Designers Paul Reid, Rebecca Johns